Word Study in Action

Words Their Way™

Big Book of **A**

Rhymes

CELEBRATION PRESS
Pearson Learning Group

Contents

Go Away, Tiger!

There is a tiger on my farm.

He never really did much harm.

His appetite is getting big.

Now he seems to like the pig.

He smiled at the goat today.

The tiger needs to go away.

Time to Shop for School

It's time to shop for school.

The jeans and watch are cool.

How about a dolphin book?

Here's one on lions, look.

There's a kangaroo, hooray!

But it's not on our list today.

A Day at the Zoo

Yesterday we went to the zoo

In our van with Val and Lou.

We waved to some yellow yaks.

Then a monkey ate our snacks.

We counted zebras one, two, three,

And heard hyenas laugh hee, hee.

The Snowman

Today we made a snowman

And rolled him very fat.

On his head we put a pan.

It made a dandy hat.

Where's My Cap?

Max lost his favorite cap.

It happened while he took a nap.

He asked his mom and dad.

But they said, "That's too bad."

Then he saw Lad's tail wag

And knew his cap was now a rag.

One Hot Day

One hot day a dog and hog

Saw a frog hop on a log.

Dog and Hog like the spot

To sit and rest when it is hot.

Frog said, "I know what to do!"

Then Dog and Hog hopped in, too.

Ben's Red Hen

Ben has a little red hen.

She can count up to ten.

Five times she kicks each leg.

Then we cheer, "Hooray for Meg."

Meg is very smart, you bet.

But she's the only hen I've met.

A Bug and a Nut

A bug saw a nut in the sun.

She tried to grab it and run.

With a push and a tug,

The nut fell on the rug.

Now the bugs are all having

Some fun!

Mr. Fig Met a Pig

Mr. Fig went up the hill

To look for his best friend, Jill.

On his way, he saw a pig.

It was wild and really big.

Mr. Fig did a flip,

And down the hill he did zip.

On Our Ship

We sail in our ship.

Over waves we skip.

There may be a chance.

We'll make it to France.

What Do You Think?

Do you think

A whale will sink

When it tries to take a drink?

Do you know why

Those fish are shy

When a shark goes swimming by?

Watch Out, Sheep!

Beep, beep!

Watch out, sheep

When Tom chugs by in his jeep.

Thump, thump!

Over a hump—

Look out, Tom, you hit a bump!

Stan Is Sad

Stan lost his top.

It didn't stop

When he had it last.

Now he is sad

And feeling bad

For losing a top so fast.

My Special Skill

I have a very special skill.

Every drink I get I spill.

I'm sure it's because I like to spin.

Turning 'round just makes me grin.

Spinning, grinning all the while,

Watching me will make you smile.

I Fly So High

I fly so high in my swing.

I'm like a bird on the wing.

My feet snag clouds in the air.

Any higher gives me a scare.

Hurry to My Place!

Hurry over to my place.

We will plan to have a race.

We can try my new blue boat,

And see if it will sink or float.

We'll go down the slippery slide.

Then take our bikes out for a ride.

The River Frog

Down by the river lives a frog.

His skin gleams green and gray.

He sits and croaks upon his log,

And clamps his jaws

On flies all day.

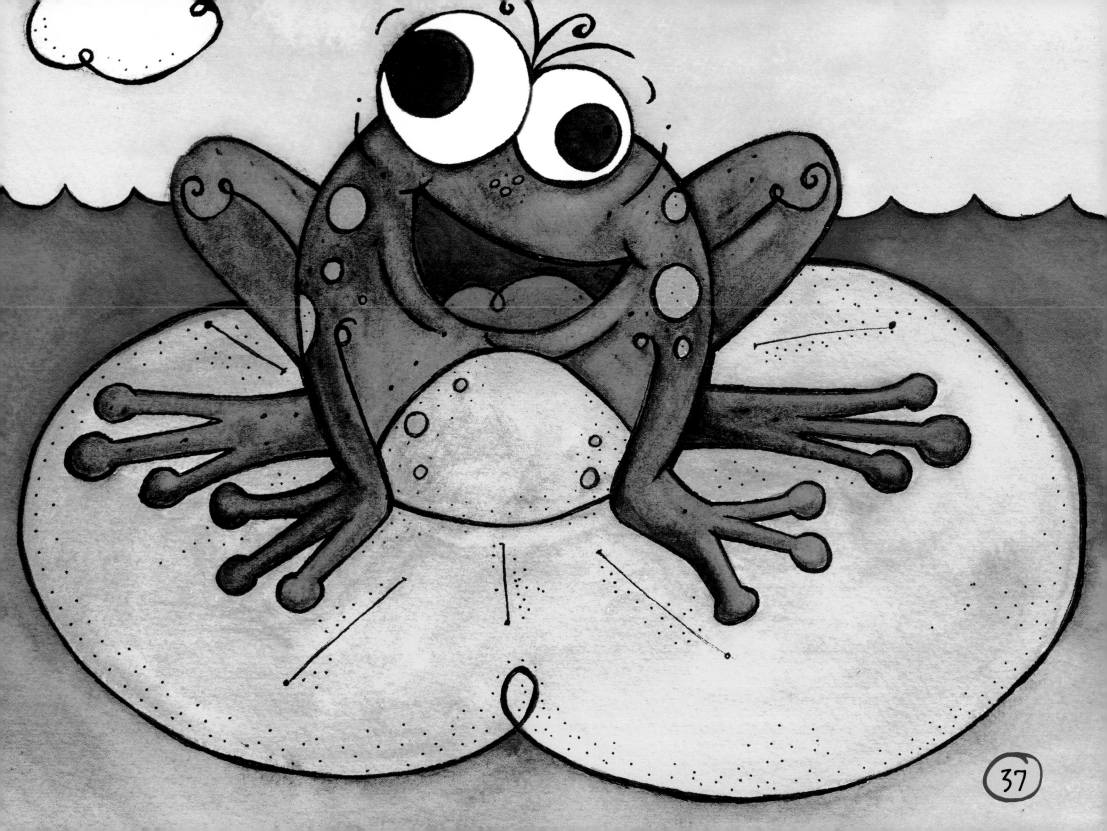

Sack Race

Let's go to the track.

We can race in a sack.

There are all kinds of prizes

In large and small sizes.

"Bravo," we'll scream

For the best dream team.

Whales Can Do Tricks

A killer whale is black and white.

We hope he doesn't bite.

The whale is big and very quick

As he performs a tricky trick.

When the trainer twirls her wrist,

The whale begins to spin and twist.

The Cat

Up climbed the cat.

On a branch she sat.

The day was hot,

But the cat was not.

It was a good fit,

So the cat stayed to sit.

A Spin and a Grin

Lin said with a grin,

"Let's go for a spin."

So Lin and Dan spun.

And they had lots of fun.

Bob's Sled

Bob is glad

The snow's so bad.

School is out for the day.

Out to the shed

To grab his red sled—

Bob will sleigh ride away.

Someday

Peg takes care of pets.

Someday she'll be a vet.

She'll help pigs and dogs

And even help some frogs.

When they feel well and snug,

She'll give them each a hug.

49

Play Ball!

Bill kicked the ball.

Jill made the call.

Nell ran well.

Their fans all yell.

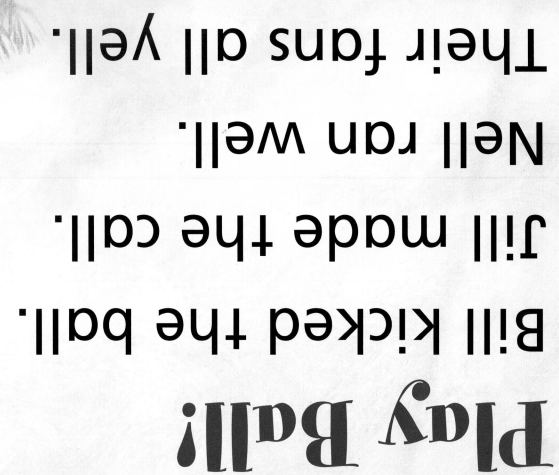

Time Talk

Snack time, chore time,

Play time, too—

Your clock tells you what to do:

"Do this now and make it quick!

Hurry! Hurry! Tick, tock, tick!

Listen to me when I chime.

It's good luck to be on time."

Dinnertime

The cook is in a rush.

The kitchen is a crush.

He's making a special dish.

He's baking a great big fish.

Oops! The pan goes crash.

Now it goes into the trash.

Jogging

An ant wanted to jog.

She ran up the road in the fog.

She slowed to a trot

When the day became hot.

Then she sat down to nap on a log.

Having Fun

Together we run.

We both have fun.

We plan our next trip

To sail a big ship.

We try on a wig

Then dance a jig.

Nighttime

See the setting sun.

The nighttime has begun.

The hen will go to rest

Upon her cozy nest.

The chicks come at a trot

To find their own soft spot.

Treasure Chest

Chen finds an old chest.

What's inside is the best.

She pulls out a ship.

One sail has a rip.

Then she sees a big shell

and thinks, "This is swell!"

Greg Packs

Greg plans for his trip.

Not a thing will he skip.

He puts clothes from his bed

In the trunk with his sled.

All the stuff he crushes

But has no spot for his brushes.

My Cow

Of all the cows mine is best.

She stands out from all the rest.

She likes a pat on her soft rump.

Then she gives a little jump.

I get pink milk from my cow.

You might wonder how.

The Trip

Meg and Dan are on a trip.

From shop to shop they skip.

Dan gets a cat named Scat.

Meg buys a big red hat.

Then they stop to eat a bun.

Meg and Dan have lots of fun.

Grapes

The grapes were on the vine.

They did look ripe and fine.

We put some on a plate.

Then all of them we ate.

Mr. Green

Early on a day in June,

Birds began to sing a tune.

Mr. Green could not sleep

When the birds began to cheep.

Every day at dawn he rose,

Then spent the day in a doze.

I Wonder

Do crocodiles sleep?

Do they ever weep?

Can they fake a smile

For a short or long while?

My goal is to find a clue

To see if those things are true.

Credits

PROGRAM REVIEWERS

Pam Brown, Teacher
Sayre School
Lexington, KY

Katrina Currier, Language Arts Curriculum Coordinator
San Francisco Day School
San Francisco, CA

Kathy Lamkin, Teacher
Tuscan Elementary School
Maplewood, NJ

Shellie Winter, Teacher
Ponce de Leon Elementary School
Clearwater, FL

The following people have contributed to the development of this product:
Art and Design: Tricia Battipede, Sherri Hieber-Day, Dorothea Fox, David Mager, Elbaliz Mendez, Judy Mahoney
Editorial: Leslie Feierstone-Barna, Linette Mathewson, Tracey Randinelli
Inventory: Yvette Higgins
Marketing: Christine Fleming
Production/Manufacturing: Alan Dalgleish
Publishing Operations: Jennifer Van Der Heide

ILLUSTRATIONS: Cover: Terry Kovalcik **Interior:** 5: Brian Lies. 7, 35: Maurie Manning. 9: Karen Lee. 11: Anthony Lewis. 13, 61: James Elston. 15: Amanda Harvey. 17, 65: Laurence Cleyet-Merle/Illustration Web. 19, 25, 57: Terry Kovalcik. 21: Bill Ledger. 23, 51: Sue Williams. 27: Rob Hefferan. 29: Amy Wummer. 31: Joann Adinolfi. 33: Terry Taylor. 37: Michelle Ciappa. 39, 59: Toby Williams. 41: Mircea Catusanu. 43, 67: Barroux. 45, 69: Linda Bronson. 47: Viviana Garofoli. 49: Diane Greenseid. 53: Chris Lensch. 55, 73: Judy Stead. 63: Stacey Schuett. 71: Gosia Mosz. 75: Emilie Chollat.

ISBN 0-7652-6756-X

Printed in the United States of America

6 7 8 9 10   08 07 06

Celebration Press
Pearson Learning Group